Text STYLES

HOW TO TELL A
Legend

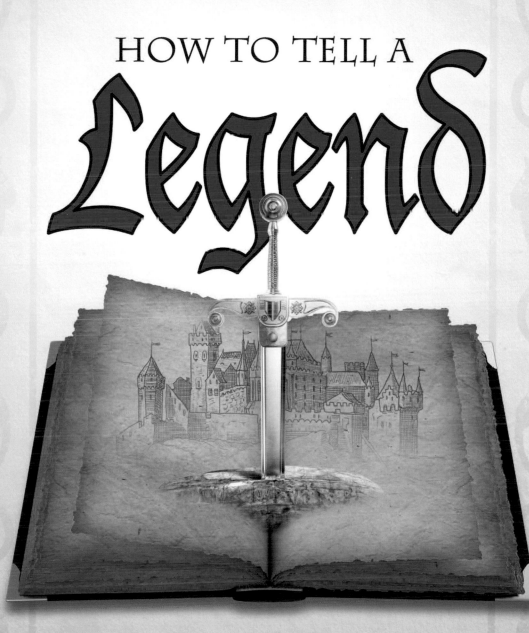

Janet Stone

 Crabtree Publishing Company

www.crabtreebooks.com

Text
STYLES

Author: Janet Stone

Coordinating editor: Reagan Miller

Publishing plan research and development:
Sean Charlebois, Reagan Miller
Crabtree Publishing Company

Editorial director: Kathy Middleton

Print coordinator: Katherine Berti

Production coordinator: Margaret Salter

Prepress technician: Margaret Salter

Logo design: Samantha Crabtree

Product development: Victory Productions, Inc.

Photo research: Tracy Vancelette

Front cover: Featured characters from legends include:
The Pied Piper of Hamelin, Johnny Appleseed, Sir Lancelot
and Isolde of the Arthurian Legends.

Title page: The magical sword called Excalibur was locked
in stone until Arthur freed it, proving himself the rightful
king. The towers of Camelot, Arthur's future castle, show
the wonders that are yet to come.

Photographs:

The Bridgeman Art Library International (Private
Collection: 18, 19

Circa Art: cover (Isolde with potion)

The Granger Collection, NYC: 5 (left)

Image Club Graphics: 10 (bottom right)

Wikimedia Commons: cover (Kate Greenaway/Project
Gutenberg eText: Pied Piper; The Grolier Society:
Sir Lancelot from The Book of Knowledge; Howe's
Historical Collections of Ohio: Johnny Appleseed)

Shutterstock: All other images

Illustrations:

Barbara Bedell: 5 & 14 (apples)

Katherine Berti: 22 (scroll and inkwell)

Bonna Rouse: 28 (bear)

Margaret Amy Salter: 27 (parchment scroll)

Cataloguing in Publication data available at Library and
Archives Canada.

Cataloging-in-Publication data available at Library of
Congress.

Crabtree Publishing Company

www.crabtreebooks.com   1-800-387-7650

Printed in Canada/082011/MA20110714

Published in Canada
Crabtree Publishing
616 Welland Ave.
St. Catharines, Ontario
L2M 5V6

Published in the United States
Crabtree Publishing
PMB 59051
350 Fifth Avenue, 59th Floor
New York, New York 10118

Published in the United Kingdom
Crabtree Publishing
Maritime House
Basin Road North, Hove
BN41 1WR

Published in Australia
Crabtree Publishing
3 Charles Street
Coburg North
VIC 3058

Contents

What is a Legend?

Johnny Appleseed, King Arthur, Robin Hood—do these people sound familiar? They are all heroes from stories called legends. A **legend** is a story from long ago that has been passed down from generation to generation. Most legends tell the story of a **hero** who performs great **feats** or good deeds. Legends are usually based on a real person or event from history. Over time, as the legend is retold, some details get changed or exaggerated. For example, a **character** may have superhuman strength or magical powers.

Cultures from around the world have legends. In some legends, the hero is a national or folk hero. Legends were often used to teach cultural values. We can learn a lot about a culture from its legends

Where do legends come from?

The first legends are thousands of years old. They began as spoken stories told to one person and passed to another. These stories were later written down. Examples of legends can be found in every culture. In some legends, the hero is a national or **folk hero**.

Why do people tell legends?

Legends are usually exciting and entertaining stories about heroes and their adventures. Legends can also teach us about the culture they come from. Very often, the heroes in legends display courage and strength. These legends inspire us.

In this book you will learn about the characteristics of legends. You will read legends and learn how to write a legend of your own!

The Legend of Johnny Appleseed

People have been telling the story of Johnny Appleseed for hundreds of years. He is an American folk hero.

John Chapman was born in Leominster, Massachusetts, in 1774. Johnny and his family lived on a farm. The family farm had good soil for growing crops. In the spring, bees buzzed around the sweet-smelling apple blossoms. Sometimes Johnny would climb up a tree to a bee hive to get a taste of the bees' honey.

"Thank you kindly for sharing your honey. I won't disturb you any longer," he would tell the bees. Johnny knew that bees worked hard for their honey. He never took more than a taste.

Johnny sure did like those apples. They were about the only sweet thing people had to eat in those days.

But as good as life was in Massachusetts, Johnny thought it was too proper. He liked being outdoors in the forests. John grew restless, and when he was a young man, he set out to explore the lands to the west. He carried with him a big bag of apple seeds that he received for free from a cider mill.

Johnny was an odd kind of fellow. He hiked up and down the hills wearing old worn-out shoes. He had to stuff the holes with leaves and hold them together with string and rags! Why, some folks didn't know what to make of him. But Johnny was friendly to the people he met, and they welcomed him into their homes. He made sleds and wagons for their children and gave bits of ribbon to the little girls.

Whenever he came to settlers' farms, he told them, "You need to plant apple trees. Apples make good eating when you pick them off a tree. You can dry them and eat them all winter long. You can make tasty apple butter and apple cider." And then he would give them some seeds to plant in their fields. Sometimes he sold seeds, or traded them for clothes. Usually, he gave the seeds away. After all, Johnny didn't need much. He lived alone in the woods and walked most everywhere he wanted to go. People saw him walking by dressed in old, raggedy clothes and wearing a pot for a hat!

Soon the Ohio Valley had a lot of apple orchards that John had planted. He took good care of them, too. But Johnny soon grew restless again. He piled bags of apple seeds into a canoe and set out for Indiana. Just as he had done in Ohio, he gave his seeds to the settlers he met. "Plant these seeds," he told them. "These seeds will grow into fine apple trees. Apples will feed you all winter long!"

Pretty soon, people began telling stories about this odd man. They started calling him Johnny Appleseed.

Many settlers shared their stories about Johnny. "Johnny cares about others, for sure. One winter a man gave Johnny some boots," said one settler. "The next time Johnny passed by, he was barefoot. The man asked what happened to the boots. Johnny said that he gave the boots away to someone who needed them more."

Said another settler, "I heard that one winter Johnny was fixin' to sleep in a cave to get out of the snow. But a bear and her cubs were already sleeping there. So Johnny says to the bear, 'I reckon I'll just have to find another place to sleep, seein' as how this cave belongs to you.'"

When Johnny was 71 years old, he got news that some cattle had broken into an apple orchard. Off he went to protect it. Sadly, his old, thin body could not take the long journey and Johnny died. To honor his memory, he was buried near one of his apple orchards.

Legendary Characters

A legend is based on a real person who lived during a particular time and place. The main character in a legend is always a hero. This hero has qualities that we admire. These qualities are called traits. A trait is part of a hero's personality that does not change. For example, a hero is usually confident. The hero may sometimes feel worried or scared, but most of the time, the hero acts boldly and confidently.

Heroes in a legend have a purpose, or mission. Johnny Appleseed wanted to plant apple trees for new settlers so they would have food to eat. Johnny believed in his cause. He was honest and hardworking. He showed determination. These character traits help us understand him.

> Look back at the legend. Which of these traits did Johnny Appleseed have?

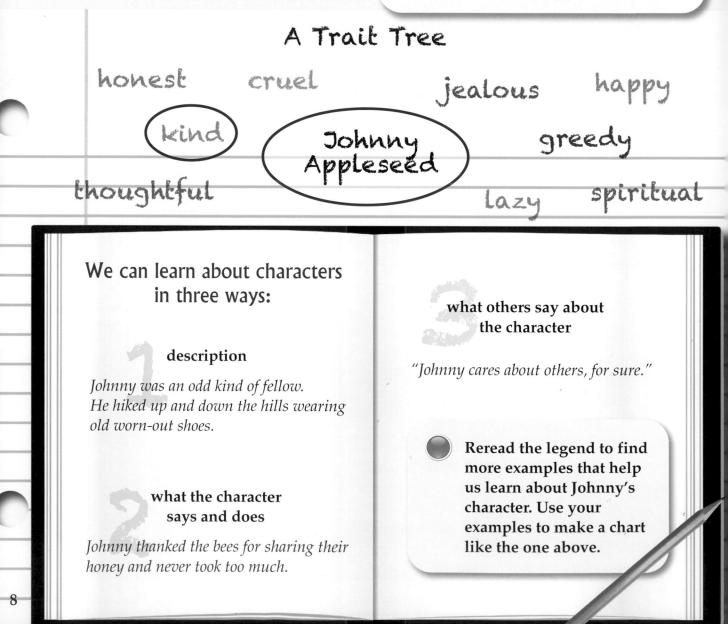

A Trait Tree

honest   cruel   jealous   happy

kind   Johnny Appleseed   greedy

thoughtful   lazy   spiritual

We can learn about characters in three ways:

1 description

Johnny was an odd kind of fellow. He hiked up and down the hills wearing old worn-out shoes.

2 what the character says and does

Johnny thanked the bees for sharing their honey and never took too much.

3 what others say about the character

"Johnny cares about others, for sure."

> Reread the legend to find more examples that help us learn about Johnny's character. Use your examples to make a chart like the one above.

Bringing a Character to Life

The legend of Johnny Appleseed tells the story of an ordinary person who did extraordinary things. We learn about Johnny's traits through his actions. We can also learn about Johnny by paying close attention to descriptions and details in the story. The passage below describes a small moment in Johnny Appleseed's life. Pay close attention to the descriptions and details.

About noontime, Johnny's stomach rumbled with hunger. He pulled some cornbread and a handful of nuts from his sack. As he bit into his cornbread, a squirrel hopped close. Johnny chuckled softly and held out a handful of nuts. "All creatures under the sky got to eat," he said.

Johnny and the squirrel made short work of this small lunch. Then Johnny went on his way, calling a good-bye to the squirrel and whistling a hymn.

What descriptions and details help teach us about Johnny's character traits?

The chart below shows us how a character's action and words can help us learn more about the character. What other details from the passage above could you add to this chart?

What a character says or does ▶	What I learned from this detail ▶
Johnny chuckled softly and held out a handful of nuts. "All creatures under the sky got to eat," he said.	Johnny is kind to animals and living things. He is generous and shares what little he has.
Johnny went on his way, calling a good-bye to the squirrel and whistling a hymn.	Johnny seems like a happy man. He whistles a hymn, which tells me that he believes in a religion.

Dialogue and Dialect: Spoken Words

The words that characters speak in a legend are called **dialogue**. Dialogue makes characters seem like real people and helps the story come alive. We can learn a lot about a character by what they say and how they say it.

Read this dialogue out loud. Can you hear Johnny's gentleness?

Dialect **is a particular way of speaking. Some people use different grammar and say words in a different way.**

"Thank you kindly for sharing your honey. I won't disturb you any longer."

"I heard that one winter Johnny was <u>fixin'</u> to sleep in a cave to get out of the snow. But a bear and her cubs were already sleeping there. So Johnny says to the bear, 'I <u>reckon</u> I'll just have to find another place to sleep, <u>seein'</u> <u>as</u> <u>how</u> this cave belongs to you.' "

The underlined words in the above passage are examples of dialect. The character pronounces words differently. Instead of saying "fixing" and "seeing," he drops the letter g at the end of the words. "I reckon" is a way of saying "I suppose" or "I think."

Johnny Appleseed would not say, "I see that this cave belongs to you." He would say "seein' as how." These word choices are important in painting a picture of a character.

It's All in How You Say It

Imagine that Johnny Appleseed was making a sled for a boy or giving ribbons to a girl. Write a conversation between Johnny and the child. Make the dialogue sound realistic by using dialect.

Setting: The *Where* and *When*

A legend takes place in a particular time and place. This time and place are the setting. The people who first told the legend wanted to honor someone who was important in their history and culture. The legend of Johnny Appleseed takes place in the early 1800s. Most of the story takes place in the Ohio Valley. Details help readers picture the time and place.

But John was friendly to the people he met, and they welcomed him into their homes. He made sleds and wagons for their children and gave bits of ribbon to the little girls.

What does this passage teach us about the time and place?

- In the 1800s, people passing by a farm were welcomed, since they often brought news.
- Most people walked to get around.
- Many wore old clothes.
- Children were happy to get a sled or some ribbons.

These small details help readers understand why the characters act, talk, and dress the way they do.

Said another settler, "I heard that one winter Johnny was fixin' to sleep in a cave to get out of the snow. But a bear and her cubs were already sleeping there. So Johnny says to the bear, 'I reckon I'll just have to find another place to sleep, seein' as how this cave belongs to you.'"

Maybe Johnny did not try to get into a bear's cave, but he could have. Bears were not such a rare sight in the 1800s, and Johnny did sleep outside. Details in a legend tell the reader something about the time and place. The details are based on fact, even though the legend may have been exaggerated.

- What other details in the legend help you picture the setting? What do they tell you about the time and place?

A Good Place for a Legend
Write details for your own setting for a legend. List details that describe where and when the story takes place. Look up information about the time and place in books or on the Internet. Use this information to help describe your setting.

Plot: The Basic Outline

The legend of Johnny Appleseed follows his life, from his birth to his death. It has a beginning, middle, and end. Johnny is the main character. He planted apple trees so that settlers would have food, and he did what he set out to do. This sums up his life in just a few sentences.

A plot **is the basic outline of a story. Legends have similar plots.**

- **A legend begins with a problem that the hero must solve.**
- **The** events **show how the hero solves the problem.**
- **The turning point, or** climax **comes when the hero solves the problem. The turning point is the most exciting part.**
- **After the turning point, or climax, the events are neatly wrapped up in a satisfying way. This part of the legend is called the** resolution.

Legends often have positive and inspiring endings. The hero often succeeds in doing what he or she sets out to do.

People added many tales to the legend about Johnny Appleseed. The following story was told and retold many times:

During the War of 1812 between the U.S. and Britain, villages in the Ohio territory were being attacked. When a town near him was attacked, Johnny Appleseed ran through the night in bare feet to warn settlers and get help.

The story map for this story about Johnny would look like this:

Problem: Johnny needs to get help.
Events:

1. Settlers learn they may be attacked.

2. They gather together in a lookout building for safety.

3. Johnny runs all night to a fort to get help.

4. Turning point: Johnny makes it to the fort at sunrise and tells soldiers to come and protect the settlers.

5. Soldiers march to the lookout building to protect the settlers.

6. Settlers go home.

Resolution: The settlers tell the story about how Johnny ran for help. The story spreads and becomes part of the legend.

• Why is the turning point the moment that Johnny reaches the fort?

Story Map
A story map can help you outline your legend.

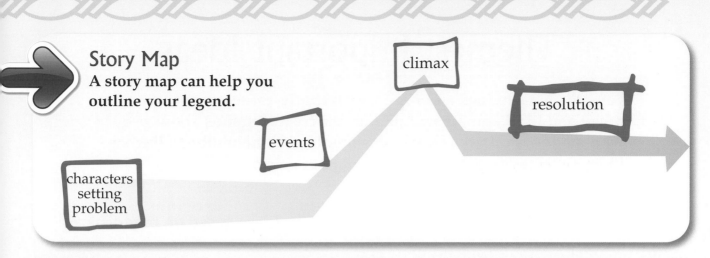

First, introduce the characters, the setting, and the problem, then write the events. The events take up most of your legend. After the climax, the legend ends quickly.

Look at this story map about one adventure of Robin Hood. Robin Hood became an outlaw when he refused to pay high taxes. He and his band of Merry Men lived in the forest. They robbed from the rich and gave to the poor. They often tricked their enemy, the Sheriff of Nottingham. This story map describes one of Robin's adventures.

Story Map for "Robin Hood Frees an Innocent Man"

Characters   Robin Hood, the Sheriff of Nottingham

Setting   a forest and small town in England around 1200 C.E.

Problem   Robin Hood must rescue a man from jail.

Events
1. An old man tells Robin Hood about a man who has been put in jail.
2. Robin Hood trades clothes with the old man to disguise himself.
3. Robin Hood asks the sheriff if he can be the jailer.
4. The sheriff is fooled and agrees to give Robin Hood the keys to the jail.
5. Robin Hood blows his horn and all his men appear.
6. Robin Hood and his men release the man from jail.

Resolution   The man joins Robin Hood and his men.

Themes: Important Ideas

Legends have heroes we admire. Everybody values people who are brave and kind and act with honor. We create legends about people who made a sacrifice or gave up something to help others. Heroes in legends have qualities we value in our culture.

Johnny Appleseed planted apple trees. In doing so, he did something important for others. The seeds he planted are still here. They are in the apple orchards that people planted using his seeds. They are in the apples we eat today.

To find the themes in the legend of Johnny Appleseed, think about his qualities we admire. Think about his generous and selfless acts.

Legends are based on big ideas, or themes, **that teach us lessons about life. The lesson can often be stated in short phrases, for example:**

- **Love is stronger than hate.**
- **Forgiving others will set you free.**
- **Follow your dreams.**

Themes of Johnny Appleseed

One person can make a difference.

Be true to yourself.

Respect nature and all living things.

Deep Meanings

Choose a favorite legend. What theme or themes can you find in it? Write the theme and explain why it is important. What life lesson does it teach?

Creative Response to the Legend

Add to the legend "Johnny Appleseed went barefoot." His feet became very tough. People said they were so tough that a rattlesnake could not bite them. Write a story about this and add it to the legend of Johnny Appleseed.

- Write dialogue that is similar to the way people spoke during that time.

- Use descriptive details—Help the reader picture the setting, characters, and action.

- Use exaggeration—When something is exaggerated, we say that it is larger than life. It is bigger, or more extreme, than anything we can find in real life.

 ## An Apple Poster

Create a poster to encourage people to plant apple trees. Use reasons from the legend. Add your own persuasive reasons and write a catchy title. Include drawings in your poster.

 ## Journal Entry

Write a personal response about the legend of Johnny Appleseed.

- What do you think of him?

- What qualities of Johnny Appleseed do you admire? Does he have qualities that you would like to develop in yourself?

The Legend of King Arthur

The Legend of King Arthur is based on a real person who lived in England hundreds of years ago. The legend grew about the king's many accomplishments. King Arthur and his knights performed brave acts. It was said they rescued maidens and fought dragons. King Arthur united the people of England and brought peace to the land.

When King Arthur died, some say his body was placed on an island called Avalon. People say that he is only sleeping and will one day rise again to rule his country.

The legend of King Arthur begins at his birth. Arthur was the son of King Uther. When Arthur was born, his father was afraid that his enemies would harm his son. He asked Merlin, a wise magician, to watch over Arthur. Merlin took Arthur away to a man named Sir Ector, who raised Arthur as though he was his own son. Arthur would not be told that his real father was King Uther until the time was right.

In "The Sword in the Stone," Arthur discovers his true identity.

The Sword in the Stone

Merlin, a wise magician, called all men of noble birth in England to come to London to participate in a *jousting* tournament. King Uther had died in battle leaving England in need of a king. The winner of the tournament would be crowned king.

When Sir Ector heard this news, he called his son, Sir Kay, and Arthur to his side. "Kay, you have trained well and hard to be a knight. I bid you come with me to London and enter the jousting tournament. You will bring honor to our family." He turned to face Arthur, who had served Sir Kay for the past years. "Arthur, you are to stay at Kay's side and assist him in the tournament."

Arthur stood tall. His heart swelled. "I will be proud to carry Sir Kay's sword and flag."

The day of the jousting tournament was bright and clear. Flags fluttered in the breeze. The benches were filled with lords and ladies dressed in richly colored robes. The knights' armor shone in the sunlight. Arthur gazed with wonder at the scene. Never had he seen such a noble sight!

As Arthur led Sir Kay in his armor toward his horse, Sir Kay drew his sword and swung it as though he was in battle. The sword hit metal and broke in two.

Sir Kay cried out in horror, "Arthur, go quickly back to our tents and get my father's sword!"

"I will go with all speed!" And off Arthur ran as fast as he could.

As he ran, he thought of a sword that he had seen in the cathedral square. This sword was stuck in a stone. "Surely it will be faster to pull that sword out of the stone than run all the way back to our tents," he thought. "I will not let Kay down. He must have a sword at once."

Arthur ran to the square and grabbed the sword. It came out smoothly and easily. A thrill went through him. He looked upon it with wide eyes, then shook himself awake. "Make haste!" he said to himself, and off he ran to Sir Kay.

"I have your sword," he panted.

When Sir Kay saw it, his face turned white. "Where did you get this sword?" he asked in a strange voice.

"I pulled it out from the stone," replied Arthur.

Sir Kay paused. How he longed to own the sword! But he kneeled before Arthur. "My lord, I am your servant."

"Nay, arise, Kay," said Arthur.

"The sword you hold is special. Hundreds of men before you have tried to free it from the stone. Look closely at the sword and you will understand."

Arthur looked at the handle and read aloud in wonder, "Whoever pulls this sword from the stone is the rightful king of England."

Sir Ector and Merlin approached. "Aye, Merlin brought you to me as a baby, away from those who might harm you. Your father was King Uther. Merlin told me to watch over you, until the time was right."

Merlin then called everyone to the square. He commanded Arthur to put the sword back in the stone and pull it out for all to see. Once, twice, three times Arthur drew the sword from the stone.

"Behold your king, Arthur, the son of King Uther!" cried Merlin.

A hush fell over the crowd, then cheers rang out. "Long live the king!" they cried.

Arthur had fulfilled his destiny to become king, and his heart lifted with joy and gladness.

Characters: Shining Examples

Heroes in legends are loyal and brave. When you read a legend, pay close attention to details. In "The Sword in the Stone," Arthur's actions provide clues about his character. Read these sentences from the story.

- *Arthur stood tall. His heart swelled. "I will be proud to carry Sir Kay's sword and flag."*

- *"I will not let Kay down. He must have a sword at once."*

- *Arthur's heart lifted with joy and gladness.*

Based on these sentences, readers can figure out that Arthur is a good and loyal person.

The moment Arthur pulled the sword from the stone, his life was forever changed. He was now the King of England. Although he was only a young man, Arthur took on this great responsibility. Arthur rose to the challenge and became a great ruler.

Which of these words below could be used to describe Arthur's traits? What other words would you use?

honest   selfish

trustworthy   modest

lazy

Main and Minor Characters

Arthur is the main character in the legend. Sir Kay is a minor character. Minor characters are not at the center of the legend. However, they give the main character a chance to speak and act. They can be important in moving the plot forward.

What kind of person is Sir Kay? How do you know?

Look at the chart below. It shows some of Arthur's traits.

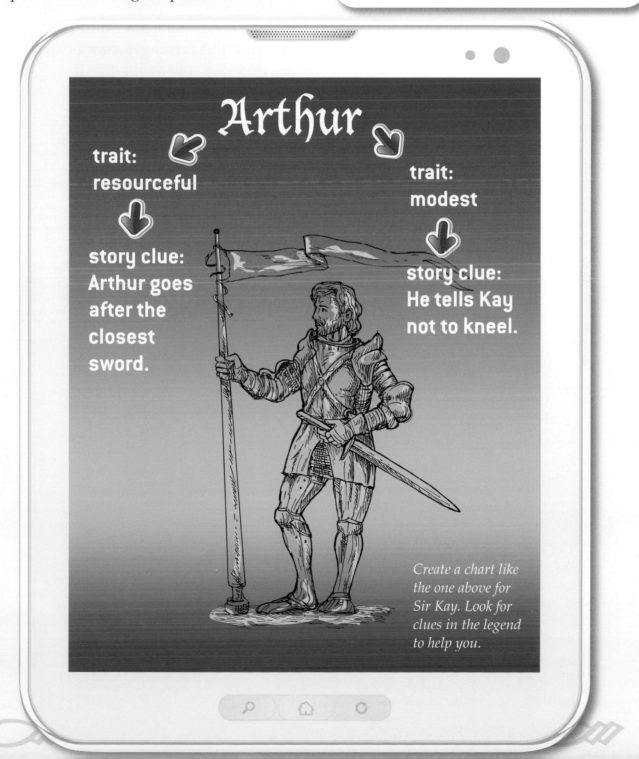

Arthur

trait:
resourceful

story clue:
Arthur goes after the closest sword.

trait:
modest

story clue:
He tells Kay not to kneel.

Create a chart like the one above for Sir Kay. Look for clues in the legend to help you.

Dialogue: Formal and Informal Words

In the legend of Johnny Appleseed, characters spoke in dialect. They sounded the way people spoke in everyday life.

In this legend, the dialogue is formal.

When Sir Ector says, "I bid you come with me," he is using formal language. He is telling Sir Kay to come with him to London.

Formal Dialogue

"I bid you come with me."

"I will go with all speed!"

"Make haste!"

Informal Dialogue

"Let's go to London together."

"I'll go as a fast as I can!"

"Hurry!"

Dialogue tells the reader what the character is thinking and feeling. Dialogue can also be used to move the action of the legend forward.

Author's Craft: Tone

The dialogue in the legend of the Sword in the Stone helps to create a serious tone, or mood.

The dialogue in the legend of Johnny Appleseed is less formal than the dialogue in the Sword in the Stone. The less formal dialogue creates a lighthearted tone, or mood.

Compare and Contrast

Imagine that King Arthur has invited Johnny Appleseed to plant an apple orchard at his castle. Write a conversation between these two characters. Remember to use formal dialogue for King Arthur and informal dialogue for Johnny Appleseed.

Setting:
When Knights Were Bold

Castles! Wise magicians! Magical swords! The legend of the Sword in the Stone is set in England in the Middle Ages. This setting is a time and place that stirs our imagination.

Arthur most likely lived around 600 C.E. in England. Life was hard in the Middle Ages. Castles were cold and dark, and many people were poor and hungry. Most legends do not include these things in the setting. Instead, the legend makes life in early England seem exciting and full of adventure.

Picture this scene in your mind. What additional details do you add? Do you see prancing horses? Do you hear trumpets? Authors use description to make the setting seem real. Then, readers use their own imaginations to add more details.

The day of the tournament was bright and clear. Flags fluttered in the breeze. The benches were filled with lords and ladies dressed in richly colored robes. Armor shone in the sunlight. Arthur gazed with wonder at the scene. Never had there been such a noble sight!

A Medieval Tournament
Draw a picture of a tournament. Include knights on horseback. Use details from this legend and the illustrations. Find out more by reading other books about the Middle Ages. Reading legends is a good way to learn about history.

The Plot Thickens!

The plot in "The Sword in the Stone" features the common characteristics found in most legends. The first part of "The Sword in the Stone" introduces us to the characters and the setting. We learned that Sir Kay travels to London to be in the jousting tournament. Arthur travels with him to help. Then, the problem is introduced. Sir Kay breaks his sword. Arthur must get him a new one quickly. This shows how minor characters, such as Sir Kay, play an important part in the plot!

A climax, or turning point, comes when Arthur pulls the magical sword out of the stone. This is a moment of great excitement.

Arthur ran to the square and grabbed the sword. It came out smoothly and easily. A thrill went through him. He looked upon it with wide eyes, and then shook himself awake.

Legends can have more than one climax. After Arthur pulls the sword from the stone, there is another moment of excitement:

Event: Arthur gives the sword to Sir Kay.
Event: Sir Kay kneels before Arthur. He calls Arthur "my lord."

Arthur learns that he is really a king! This is another climax. The rest of the action leads to the resolution.

Event: Merlin and Sir Ector tell Arthur about his father.
Event: Arthur pulls the sword out again in front of everyone.

Resolution: Arthur fulfills his destiny to become king.

Theme: Ideas to Live by

The themes of truth and honor are at the heart of many legends. Knights in legends fight for truth and honor, and follow a code of honor.

- In "The Sword in the Stone," how does Sir Kay show the theme of "truth and honor"?

- How does Arthur show the theme of "do your best"?

Themes of Legends

The themes in the legend of Johnny Appleseed teach us these lessons:

- Respect nature
- Be kind
- Help others

The themes in the legend of the Sword in the Stone teach us these lessons:

- Rise to a challenge
- Act with loyalty
- Be honest

Doing the Right Thing Is Its Own Reward

Sir Kay almost wanted to keep the sword for himself. But he knew that it belonged to Arthur. Tell about a time when you had to make a decision. You may not have wanted to do something, but you knew it was the right thing to do. Write about your experience.

Creative Response to the Legend

Certificate of Knighthood

Sir Kay was honest; Sir Ector was kind. Do you know a person with these traits? Create a certificate of knighthood to award this person. Roll up the certificate and tie it with a ribbon to make it look like a scroll.

A Coat of Arms

Knights carried shields. They used colors and symbols on their shields to stand for their family, their values, and their traits. For example, a bear on a coat of arms stood for strength. Create your own coat of arms. Use symbols that stand for things that are important to you.

You Are There

Imagine that you were in the square and saw Arthur pull the sword from the stone. Write a diary entry. Include details about the setting and the action. Make the moment come alive. How did you feel? Did you cheer with the others?

Writing a Legend

1 Prewriting

Choose a Topic

Choose a legend to retell or write your own.

A legend begins with a hero. Who will your hero be? Write down characters you can use as the hero of your legend. Think of a character who is strong and brave. Or, start with a character who might become a hero by doing a great deed.

Look at the scroll on the right. Does one of these characters spark your imagination? Add your own ideas to the list.

Legends Based on Real People
Davy Crockett
Robin Hood

Characters Waiting to Become Legends
Plain Jane Magillicutty
Sir Dance-a-lot

2 Explore Your Hero

What makes your character special? Is your character smart and clever? Will she need to use her cleverness and quick mind to solve a problem or do something special? Or does your character rely on courage and strength? Heroes in legends are "larger than life." Exaggerate the character's traits.

3 Problems! Problems!

A good hero needs something to fight or a problem to solve. Start with a good problem for your hero to face. Does your hero have to rescue a maiden? Does he have to deliver an important message? How will your character solve this problem? Write the main events. One event may lead you to another. Let your ideas flow!

How will your legend end? Will the hero win the fight? Will good triumph over evil? Of course!

A Good Lesson
Legends are written to entertain and inspire. Think about the lesson you want readers to learn.

4 Write a First Draft

Write your first draft. Do not worry about making mistakes. Just get your ideas down on paper and use your notes. Include the key events in a story map. But if your ideas take you in a different direction, follow them! The best ideas will come while you are writing.

Keep these questions in mind:

- **Why did people tell stories about your hero?**
- **What great deed did your hero do?**
- **What kind of dialogue would your hero speak?**
- **What details will help make your hero seem real to the reader?**

Hector decided to write about Davy Crockett. His first draft is short because he is just getting started. He has included his main character, the problem, some main events, and a possible solution.

> The Legend of Davy Crockett
>
> Davy Crockett was a real smart man. He knew all about the woods.
>
> One time he met a bear. The bear was really big and growled at Davy.
>
> Davy circled around the bear. Then he grabbed the bear in a big hug. Why, he hugged that bear so tight that the bear just fell down.
>
> "Now you just go along," said Davy. "Your cubs are looking for you."

Revise Your Legend

Read your legend aloud. Find parts that can be improved.

- Does it have details about the time and place?
- Does it have dialogue?
- Does it have actions that show what the hero is like?

Make changes to your legend

Hector added some descriptive details about Davy. He added details about the setting.

The Legend of Davy Crockett

Davy Crockett was a real smart man. He knew all about the woods. He didn't have to go to school to learn everything there was to know.

One time he was out cutting a trail in the Tennessee woods and he met a bear. The bear was twice as tall as Davy and growled at Davy.

Davy acted like he wasn't scared. "Howdy, bear," said Davy. "There's no need for you to get so mad. I ain't goin' to harm you."

Davy circled around the bear. Then he grabbed the bear in a big hug. Why, he hugged that bear so tight that the bear just fell down!

6 Proofread Your Draft

Now reread your legend. Fix any mistakes.

- **Did you use quotation marks around dialogue?**
- **Did you use capital letters for the names?**
- **Did you spell all words correctly?**

7 Make a Final Copy

Copy your legend neatly on a new piece of paper. Add a title. Hector continued to work on his legend. Here is his final copy.

Think of ways to share your writing:

- Make a cover for your story. Draw a picture that has details about the setting
- Read your legend aloud to your family and friends

The Legend of Davy Crockett

Davy Crockett was a real smart man. He knew all about the woods. He didn't have to go to school to learn everything there was to know.

One time, he was out cutting a trail in the Tennessee woods. All of a sudden, he met a bear. That bear was twice as tall as Davy. It growled at Davy.

Davy acted like he wasn't scared. "Howdy, bear," said Davy. "There's no need for you to get so mad. I ain't goin' to harm you."

Davy grabbed the bear in a big hug. The bear fell down. Davy and that bear rolled down the trail and back up again. Davy hugged that bear until the bear got tired.

"Whew!" said Davy. "What a big bear hug!" And from that time on, everybody knew that Davy was goin' to be the king of the wild frontier.

Proofreading Symbols

delete
bearrs

replace   squirrels
~~foxes~~

make upper case
CAP davy Crockett

insert big
a hug

Glossary

character	A person or animal in a story
climax	The point of greatest excitement or tension
dialect	The way people of a particular region speak
dialogue	Exact words spoken by characters
event	Action that happens in a legend
feats	Acts of great courage or skill
first person	A story is told by the main character, using the word
folk hero	Someone who is admired for their achievements by the people in a particular place
hero	The most important character in a legend
jousting	A sporting event in which knights on horseback charge at each other carrying large poles and try to knock their opponent off their horse
legend	A story about a real person who lived in a particular time and place
plot	The basic outline of a story or legend
resolution	The part of the story that shows how the problem or conflict is solved
setting	The time and place in which a story unfolds
story map	A diagram that shows the basic parts of the plot
theme	Main idea or message of a tale

Index

Further Resources

Books:

How the Stars Fell into the Sky: A Navajo Legend by Jerri Oughton. Sandpiper Publishing (1996)

Weather Legends: Native American Lore and the Science of Weather by Carole G. Vogel. Lerner Publishing Group (2001)

Legends of the Sea by Adrian Vigliano. Heinemann-Raintree (2010)

The Legend Of Sleepy Hollow by Washington Irving. Ideals Publications (2008)

The Legend of the Loon by Kathy-Jo Wargin. Sleeping Bear (2003)

The Ride: The Legend of Betsy Dowdy by Kitty Griffin. Atheneum (2010)

Websites:

This site features retellings of popular legends from North America.
americanfolklore.net/folklore/myths-legends/

This site explores the legend of El Dorado.
science.nationalgeographic.com/science/archaeology/el-dorado/